The Carolina Heelsplitter in the Carolinas

Our Natural Heritage

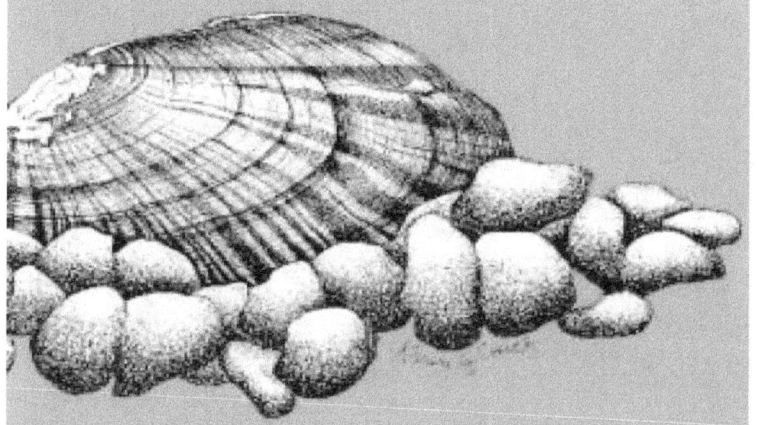

Freshwater mussels are found in rivers, lakes and streams all over the world. North America has more freshwater mussels species (nearly 300!) than any other continent. The majority of these species are found throughout the Southeastern United States. North and South Carolina alone have over 100 mussel species. Of these, almost half are considered threatened or endangered.

The Carolina Heelsplitter

A Hidden Treasure

The Carolina heelsplitter (Lasmigona decorata) is the most critically endangered mussel species of the Carolinas. The U.S. Fish and Wildlife Service (USFWS) designated the Carolina heelsplitter as a federally endangered species in 1993. Jointly, the USFWS Partners for Fish and Wildlife Program, the North Carolina Wildlife Resources Commission (NCWRC), cooperators and volunteers created this booklet to provide information on how you can help protect a part of the Carolina's natural heritage.

Lifecycle

The Carolina heelsplitter has a greenish brown to dark brown shell with yellow rays, and a pearly white to blue white nacre (inside surface).

Carolina heelsplitters

Like other freshwater mussels of the Carolina's, the Carolina heelsplitter feeds by siphoning and filtering food particles, such as algae, plankton, and bacteria, from the water. Mussels respire the same way by absorbing oxygen from the water with their gills.

The reproductive cycle of the Carolina heelsplitter begins when the male releases sperm into the water. When taken in by the female during siphoning, her eggs become fertilized and she carries them in her gills until the larvae (called glochidia) are fully developed. The female then releases the glochidia into the water where they must quickly attach to the fins or gills of a particular "fish host." The glochidia receive nourishment and oxygen from the fish, without harming it, for several weeks until they develop into juvenile mussels. The fish also serves as a vehicle for the juvenile mussels for travel to farther reaches of the stream. In this way, mussels can establish new populations.

Once the juvenile mussel is fully developed, it will drop from the fish and settle to the bottom of the stream. If habitat conditions are good, the young mussel will begin its adult life.

Fish Host

Juvenile

Glochidia

Adult

The Discovery!

The first recorded discovery of the Carolina heelsplitter was in 1852. The largest recorded specimen measured nearly five inches across. Historical geographical records from the 1800's reveal that the Carolina heelsplitter once thrived in many streams and rivers of the Pee Dee, Catawba, Savannah, and Saluda River systems in North and South Carolina. Recent surveys, however, conclude that the mussel now exists

Goose Creek

Waxhaw Creek

Lynches River

Gills Creek
Flat Creek

Cuffeytown Creek
Mountain Creek
Turkey Creek
Beaverdam Creek

Present distribution of Carolina heelsplitter (in red)

in only a small fraction of its initial known range. There are six surviving Carolina heelsplitter populations: two in North Carolina and four in South Carolina.

Home Sweet Home!
Although the Carolina heelsplitter once lived in large rivers and streams, the remaining populations are found in relatively shallow streams (one to four feet deep). The water must be clean, free flowing (unobstructed by dams or culverts) have a high-oxygen content (usually created by riffles and small rock falls), and an abundant food supply of microscopic plants and organisms.

Unstable streambank

Mussel Habitat Checklist

- clean water
- lots of oxygen
- plenty of food
- stable streambanks

A stable stream bank is also an important element of the mussel's habitat. A stable streambank is characterized by having trees and vegetation with extensive root systems that help to hold the soil of the streambank in place. Vegetation along streambanks provides shade for the stream and help moderate water temperatures during hotter months. Plants and soils also act as natural filters to help protect the stream against pollutants. Decaying leaf litter and plant material provide a vital food resource for organisms in the stream. Maintaining a wide riparian buffer has several benefits! It helps maintain an aquatic ecosystem and provides a corridor for wildlife such as birds, mammals, amphibians and reptiles. It also helps protect our water quality.

Stable
streambank

Threats

Habitat disturbance and water quality
degradation are the leading causes for
the decline of the Carolina heelsplitter
populations. Over 100 years of
urbanization in the Charlotte area
altered stream and wetland habitats.
For example, waterways were
channelized and floodplains filled. In
rural areas, best management
practices for agriculture and forestry
were unknown. All of these factors
have had significant impacts on the
water quality of local streams.

Studies have shown that freshwater
mussels, particularly juvenile
mussels, are very sensitive to water
pollutants such as oil, gas, fertilizers,
heavy metals, pesticides and other
chemicals. Over time, these
pollutants build up on our highways,
driveways, lawns, and streets, where
they become available to be washed
into nearby streams during a rain.
Rain that moves across these
surfaces is called storm water (rain
or melting snow that does not get
absorbed into the ground or captured
by trees and plants). Asphalt, roofs,
and compact soil are examples of
impermeable surfaces that prevent
rain from naturally infiltrating into
the ground.

Excessive sediment

Habitat alteration such as channelization, impoundments, or stream dredging activities eliminate mussel habitat directly, while nearby land clearing and disturbance activities enable pollutants, especially sediment, to reach streams. Excessive sediment (soil that has been eroded from land into water) in streams degrades water quality, smothers aquatic habitat, clogs fish and mussel gills, and cuts off needed sunlight to underwater plant growth.

To Live and Let Live

You may be asking yourself, "Why should I be concerned about a cold and clammy animal that lives in the bottom of streams?" There are lots of reasons! Most importantly, mussels are indicators of water quality, and we know that their peril is due in part to polluted water. Poor water quality should be a concern of everyone because it harms not only the health of animals that depend on the stream, but human health too! We rely on surface water for drinking, irrigation, fishing, and recreation.

Native mussels also play an important role in the 'web of life' where all living things are interconnected. Mussels eat small plants and organisms like bacteria, algae, and plankton, while other animals like the muskrat, raccoon, and otter in turn depend on mussels for food.

© Ken Taylor

The Carolina heelsplitter is native to the Carolinas and is found nowhere else on earth. We can be proud of this unique natural heritage feature.

The best way that you can help protect the Carolina heelsplitter and other aquatic wildlife is to keep our water clean and our streambanks undisturbed. The following chapters are a guide to help you understand how our developing landscape, and our daily activities affect the water quality of our local streams. When you practice environmental stewardship around your home, you are also protecting water quality and that is a healthy outcome we can all live with!

Water Pollution

Top: stormwater runoff; below: common household pollutants

Most of us blame water pollution on industries and corporations. In reality, we are all responsible. While a significant amount of water pollution can be directly linked to industrial plants, much of the pollution comes from many other sources—nonpoint source or runoff pollution. But what is nonpoint source pollution? It is the eroded soil from a new construction site. It is the spilled paint from your neighbor's house painting project. It is the detergent you used to wash your car (and the oil that drips from it). It is the lawn treatment you paid for. When it rains, all this and much more washes into ditches or storm sewers under our streets and travels directly (untreated by sewage treatment plants) into streams.

NC Wildlife Resources Commission

Common Household Products that Contribute to Water Pollution

- Ammonia-based cleaners
- Car waxes
- Chlorine bleach
- Chrome and silver polish
- Concrete or wood sealant
- Degreasers
- Detergents with phosphates
- Drain cleaners
- Furniture strippers and varnishes
- Lawn-care chemicals (pesticides & fertilizers)
- Mothballs
- Motor oil, gasoline, antifreeze, brake fluid, transmission fluid
- Paint and brush cleaners
- Paints, paint thinners
- Roach and ant killers
- Toilet, tub & tile cleaners

Watch the next time it rains, and see the water run off your roof, over your lawn, across your driveway and street. See the rain pick up the oil, grease, litter, soil, and other pollutants. Eventually this runoff carries them to nearby streams, where these pollutants can kill fish, shellfish, wildlife, plants, and degrade water quality.

Not all pollutants are visible however. Nutrients, dissolved metals, bacteria, and pesticides for example cannot be seen with the eye, but are just as damaging. For example, nitrogen and phosphorus found in soaps and fertilizers are a serious threat to water quality. Once these nutrients reach the water, they cause sudden and excessive growth of algae and aquatic plants. That seems like a good thing right? Wrong! When these plants die and decay, they deplete the dissolved oxygen in the water needed by fish and other aquatic life and causes instant 'kills'.

All of us in our everyday activities are to some extent polluters. The amount of pollutants may seem negligible, but multiplied by the millions of acres, lots, and homes across the Carolinas, they create a significant problem for our water resources.

Preventing Water Pollution At Home
Most of us live in areas that are characterized by acres of impervious surfaces. Think of your streets, sidewalks, and driveways as the "Stormwater Pathway." Whatever drips, spills, pours, falls, or is washed onto these surfaces will eventually find its way to a nearby stream. Reducing runoff and increasing water infiltration is a good way to limit contamination of our waters.

This may mean changing the way we care for our cars, fertilize our lawns, or landscape our yards.

Reducing Runoff
You can reduce runoff by direct downspouts to permeable areas, such as lawn, trees and landscaping; and limiting the amount of water you apply to your yard.

Permeable Pavements
The best way to reduce runoff is to limit the amount of paved or otherwise impervious surface on your property. Whenever possible, favor green space and natural ground cover. If you must pave an area, many other materials provide the durability of concrete while allowing some rainwater to filter down into the ground.

The Yard and Lawn

Landscaping to Benefit the Environment AND You
The most common mistakes homeowners make when landscaping their yards are (1) buying plants and grasses that are not well suited to the climate, soil, or location (non-native); or (2) selecting plants and grasses that require large amounts of fertilizer to grow in poor soil.

To protect water quality and save money, choose plants that are suited to your area such as native plants. Native plants grow naturally in your region and will generally withstand common diseases and insect problems far better than non-native plants, and will eliminate the need for special care and extensive watering. Native plants also provide food and shelter for visiting wildlife!

You could even convert a portion of your yard into wildlife habitat. The National Wildlife Federation (see Helpful Programs and Services at the back of this booklet) has an excellent program designed to help you get started. Several specific guidelines can help you achieve a good aesthetic effect and protect the environment:

Examples of Permeable Pavements

- bricks,
- interlocking pavers,
- flat stones (flagstone, bluestone, or granite),
- gravel,
- crushed shells or stone,
- bark chips, and
- precise concrete lattice pavers

are all examples of alternative surfaces. (And instead of relying of chemicals to control weeds between pavers, you can plant native mint or moss!)

Native
landscaping

- Locate deciduous trees (trees that lose their leaves in the winter) to shade planting beds and outdoor seating areas.

- Limit the amount of grass to areas that will be used for play, recreation, etc.

- Group together plants with similar sun, moisture, and soil requirements.

- In dry sites choose drought-tolerant and drought-resistant plant species.

- Group and limit the use of plants that need more water, placing them only in naturally wet areas.

- Mulch or compost planting beds to conserve soil moisture, control weeds, and to improve soil conditions.

- If you live near a stream, maintain a forested riparian buffer.

Around Your Yard ...
The way you landscape and care for your yard can reduce the pollution transmitted to streams. Environmentally sound watering and fertilizing—as well as strategic selection and placement of trees, plants and gardens—can limit runoff and the hazardous chemicals contained in it.

Establishing and maintaining a healthy yard with a variety of plants, shrubs, and trees not only make a home more attractive and valuable, it also has important environmental benefits.

A healthy yard:

- Moderates summer heat;

- Helps prevent erosion;

- Acts as a filter for rainwater from roofs, downspouts, and driveways;

- Minimizes dust;

- Provides food and habitat for wildlife, and

- Helps clean the air.

Having a healthy yard does not always mean having the greenest yard on the block. It means understanding and meeting the needs of your plants. Different plants require different amounts of nutrients like nitrogen and phosphorous (fertilizer) in order to grow healthy. Some plants require more than others do. Applying more nutrients than a plant can use results in excessive nutrient loading that can lead to water pollution problems as well as damage to your plants.

Consider Home Composting!
How can you use up grass clippings and yard waste, and save money and protect the environment at the same time? Home composting! Waste disposal sites in the Carolinas are filling up and are being closed down at an alarming rate. Twenty percent of the solid waste placed in landfills consists of yard and garden wastes such as leaves and grass clippings. North Carolina has banned these wastes from landfills.

When mixed with soil, compost increases the organic matter content, improves the physical properties of the soil (especially of our Carolina

Mary Staub
Composting bins

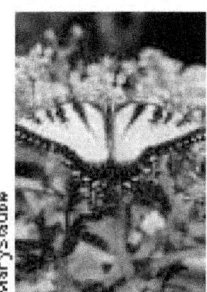

Mary Staubk

Swallowtail
butterfly

clay!), and supplies essential nutrients, enhancing the soil's ability to support plant growth. Compost can also be applied to the soil surface to conserve moisture, control weeds, reduce erosion, improve appearance, and moderate soil temperatures.

Compost is an environmentally friendly alternative to applying fertilizer. You can replace twenty percent of the nutrients supplied by the conventional fertilizer you use now with compost. That means saving money too! Ask your Cooperative Extension Service for a booklet on how to manage yard waste through composting.

Insects

Insects are considered by most people to be harmful. When in fact, 90 percent of the insects in your yard are beneficial! Too often homeowners apply a full spectrum "kill all" insecticide that eradicates both the good and the bad bugs. If you suspect a pest problem:

- Before choosing a strategy, examine the yard closely and identify the pest to determine what kind of remedy is really needed.

- Consider a variety of natural solutions, even though this may mean accepting some imperfections in the appearance of your yard.

- If chemical controls must be applied, insecticidal soap is less toxic than conventional insecticides and can kill aphids, fleas, and other pests.

- Always read the labels on the pesticides containers and their ingredients before you buy any chemicals lawn treatment products.

- Buy only the amount you plan to use.

Purple martins

Encourage beneficial insects to do the dirty work of pest control!

Beneficial insects perform vital functions and consume large numbers of pest insects. Beneficial insects work to:

- Build the soil
- Decompose organic matter
- Pollinate crops
- Eat weeds
- Provide food for other insects, birds, and reptiles

Beneficial Insects and the Pests They Control

- Damsel Bugs control aphids, leaf hoppers, mites, psyllids
- Ladybugs control aphids, aphid larvae, rootworms, weevils
- Stingless Parasitic Wasps control aphids, gypsy moths, caterpillars, cutworms
- Green Lacewings control aphids, white flies
- Spiders control Bees, treehoppers, flies, carrot weevils

Attract Insect Eating Birds and Bats

Birds and bats have high energy requirements and need to eat a lot of food. For example, six to eight bats will consume 10,000 flying insects each night. You can attract birds and bats to your yard by doing the following:

- Install bird and bat houses on your property.
- Use groundcovers instead of grass. The leaves that will build up under the groundcover provide an excellent hunting ground for birds.
- Plant native trees and vegetation of varying heights to accommodate birds and bats with different feeding and nesting habits.
- Plant shrubs and trees that produce berries.

Woodthrush

If You Must Use Pesticides...

Use your common sense when storing and disposing of pesticides. The power and persistence of chemicals should not be underestimated. Following the procedures outlined here will help protect your family, your pets, and your environment.

- Store unused chemicals in a sturdy, well-ventilated area that has a cement floor and is separate from living space. The storage area should also be insulated, keep chemicals out of direct sunlight, and secure from children and animals.

- The best way to avoid having to dispose of leftover pesticides is to buy or mix only as much as you need for one application.

- Never bury, burn or pour pesticides into storm drains or toilets.

- Give any unused chemicals to neighbors in clearly marked containers.

- If you must dispose of pesticide, read the disposal instruction.

- Some communities have hazardous waste collection programs where they will pick up chemicals once a year. If none exists in your town, find out the collection site nearest you to dispose of the chemicals yourself.

- If leaks or spills happen, never hose them down. Instead, surround the contaminated area with dirt or sprinkle an absorbent like sawdust or kitty litter on the spill. Then shovel or sweep the absorbent into a plastic bag and take to your community's hazardous waste collection site.

Toads/Frogs control flying insects, snails, slugs

Big-eyed Bugs control insect eggs, leaf hoppers, small caterpillars, Mexican bean beetles

Assassin Bugs control Colorado potato beetle, potato beetle, leaf hoppers, mites, psyllids

Syrphid Fly control plant lice (aphids)

Birds/Bats control grubs, caterpillars, mosquitoes, flying insects

Low Toxicity Pest Controls

- Insecticidal soap: Potassium salt-based, it effectively controls aphids, red spider mites, and mealy bugs. It must be applied to the pest directly.

- Soft soap: Mild dish soap (1 cup/10 gallons of water) can control aphids, red spider mites, army worms.

- Pyrethrum: Derived from the chrysanthemum plant, it is effective against most insects, especially aphids, but will also kill beneficial insects if not sprayed directly on the pest.

Caring for Your Lawn

As beautiful as an immaculate lawn may be to some, it represents an enormous investment of time, energy, and money! With over 20 million acres of lawn in America, we spend an amazing $6 billion a year to keep them green and weed-free, in addition to the fact that we use nearly half of our municipal water for watering our lawns.

Consider these alternatives to reduce your lawn maintenance.

- Plant native species as groundcover instead of grass.

- Plant trees and shrubs.

- Create a water garden or pond.

- Create a rock garden or mulched path.

- Plant annual or perennial beds.

- Establish a meadow or prairie patch with native warm season grasses and wildflowers.

- Use hedgerows.

- Create an organic vegetable garden.

- Establish a butterfly or hummingbird garden.

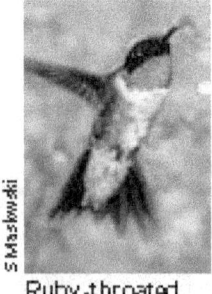

S Maslowski

Ruby-throated hummingbird

Mary Stauble

Oakleaf
hydrangea

Overall management of lawns

- Choose grass that does well in your region. Each grass types require different combinations of fertilizers, pesticides, water, and mowing.

- Have your soil tested by Cooperative Extension to find out what it needs for your plants to grow healthy. A clay soil needs organic matter worked into it, not fertilizer.

- Spread lime on acidic soil. Limestone is a natural mineral and will not pollute water but should be used and handled according to instructions.

- Aerate your soil two or three times a year or as needed to alleviate soil compaction and to increase its capacity to infiltrate water.

- Never, ever dump grass or other organic matter in or on the banks of streams.

If you must fertilize...

- Use only fertilizers formulated specifically for lawns. Garden fertilizers, for example, will not provide proper nutrients.

- Apply fertilizer only when needed, and at the proper time and amounts according to the instructions and your soil test.

The wrong fertilizer applied at the wrong time can cause disease and weeds, promote poor root growth, or excessive top growth. Incorrect fertilization can reduce your lawn's ability to withstand extreme temperatures and moisture. Adding too much fertilizer can burn your lawn rather than make it greener. And remember that a good rain can wash that excessive fertilizer off your lawn and into the stream where it can seriously damage aquatic ecosystems.

- Avoid leaving fertilizer on sidewalks or driveways where it can easily be washed into storm drains and streams.

- Use slowly soluble natural fertilizers such as blood meal, feather meal, wheat germ, soya, muriate of potash, enzymes, and soil microorganisms.

- Avoid using fertilizers within 75 feet of water.

- Do not fertilize if a rain is predicted.

Clean up after your pets

Pet feces left on the ground can be washed into the water, causing bacterial and viral contamination and boosting nutrient levels. It is best to dispose of pet feces in the trash or to flush them down the toilet.

Coping with weeds

All lawns have weeds, whether herbicides are used on them or not. That is because many different kinds of plants normally live together in nature. Trying to keep just one type of plant established in an area and all others out is literally working against nature. The trick to maintaining a lawn is to accept a "tolerance level" of weeds, keeping them low enough so that the grass is still attractive and healthy.

■ A significant weed problem may be the result of soil compaction, too much or too little fertilizer, a watering problem, or pH imbalance.

■ Crabgrass can be effectively controlled with a pre-emergence crabgrass herbicide when applied before the grass germinates. Broadleaf weeds often only need to be spot-treated.

■ Pull weeds by hand when you can.

Watering

Over-watering is the most common mistake people make when caring for their lawn. Lawns need watering when they have a bluish cast or when you can see your footprints after walking across them. An established or mature lawn should only be watered during very dry periods, and in the manner described below.

Using grass clippings, mulch, leaves, pine needles, cocoa hulls, hay, and wood chips to cover the ground. It will help prevent evaporation and keep the plant roots cool.

Minimize using sprinklers as they waste water through evaporation. Drip irrigation is the most efficient system for watering your landscaped areas. This method can cut the amount of water you use in the yard by half! A rubber soaker hose is also a good watering system.

- Water either early in the morning or after sunset to reduce loss from evaporation.

- Moisten the soil to a depth of four to six inches (this usually requires using about 3/4 to 1 inch of water). Frequent shallow watering on established grass causes shallow rooting, and invites crabgrass, and encourages disease.

- Aim sprinkler heads away from paved surfaces to avoid runoff. You have watered too much if your lawn is draining excess water into the street or drainage ditch.

Mowing

Mowing is crucial to the health of your lawn. Bluegrass or fescue should be cut to two to four inches in height and cut frequently enough that no more than a third of the leaf area is removed. Bermuda and zoysia should be mowed when they reach a height of one-half to one inch. And remember, grass clippings should never be dumped in or near streams! Grass clippings should be recycled on your lawn, reserved for pick up by your local collection facility, or you can use them in your home compost.

A Word About Lawn Care Services

Many people do not want to worry about buying and applying the right fertilizer and pesticides for their lawns. A popular alternative is to contract with a lawn service. It is strongly recommended however that you consider the pros and cons associated with this choice. You want a lawn care service that will tailor to the specific needs of your lawn, not just apply fertilizers and chemicals on a rigid schedule whether your lawn actually needs them or not. It wastes your money and can lead to water pollution!

So if you choose to use a lawn care service:

- Request natural lawn care methods rather than those that rely solely on chemical approaches.

- Study the lawn care companies' management practices.

- Have your soil tested before unnecessary fertilizers and chemicals are applied.

- Ask to see all the labels of all pesticides products they intend to use on your lawn and ask about amounts that will be applied and precautions that will be followed.

Everyone Can Be An Environmental Steward!

The quality of our water depends on the wise use of our land and natural resources by communities and individuals alike. A healthy environment insures clean water and protects the lives of people and wildlife. You and your neighbors (including the Carolina heelsplitter!) will benefit from your effort to protect our water resources.

This brochure was made possible by an educational grant from the Partners for Fish and Wildlife Program, Savannah-Santee-Pee Dee Ecosystem Team, and inkind services from the NCWRC and the USFWS.

Goose Creek

NC Wildlife Resources Commission

Helpful Programs and Services

North Carolina Wildlife Resources Commission
Division of Wildlife Management
1724 Mail Service Center
Raleigh, NC 27699-1724
Telephone: 919/661 4872
www.ncwildlife

Laura Fogo

Catawba Lands Conservancy
105 West Morehead Street
Charlotte, NC 28202
Telephone: 704/342 3330
clands@bellsouth.net
www.catawbalands.org

The Land Trust for Central North Carolina
P.O. Box 4284
Salisbury, NC 28145-4284
Telephone: 704/647 0302

Mecklenburg County Department
of Solid Waste Management
700 North Tryon Street
Charlotte, NC 28202
Telephone: 704/336 5359
(Excellent program called PLANT on reducing yard
waste, conserving water, and using native plant species
in the Piedmont.)

National Wildlife Federation
Backyard Wildlife Habitat Programs
8925 Leesburg Pike
Vienna, VA 22184
Telephone: 703/790 4434
www.nwf.org/habitats

The North Carolina Wildlife Federation
1204 The Plaza, Suite 2
Charlotte, NC 28205
Telephone: 704/377 4696
ncwf_charlotte@mindspring.com

The South Carolina Wildlife Federation
2711 Middleburg Drive, Suite 104
Columbia, SC 29204
Telephone: 803/256 0690
mail@scwf.org
(Excellent resource for wildflower, butterfly, and
native plant gardening!)

National Audubon Society
North Carolina State Office
410 Airport Road
Chapel Hill, NC 27514
Telephone/fax: 919/929 3899
www.ncaudubon.org or www.audubon.org

Natural Resource Conservation Service
4405 Bland Road, Suite 205
Raleigh, NC 27609
Telephone: 919/873 2124

North Carolina Cooperative Extension Service
Union County Center
500 North Main Street, Room 506
Monroe, NC 28112-4796
Telephone: 704/283 3742
www.ces.ncsu.edu

South Carolina Agricultural Extension Service
Clemson University Cooperative Extension Service
Clemson University
Clemson SC 29634
Telephone: 864/656 3382
www.clemson.edu/public/
(To find your local county agent,
call or look up Extensions and Personnel list)

Pee Dee National Wildlife Refuge
Route 1, Box 92
Highway 52 North
Wadesboro, NC 28170
Telephone: 704/694 5334
Laura_Fogo@fws.gov
(Partners for Fish and Wildlife Program)

U.S. Fish & Wildlife Service/ Asheville Field Office
160 Zillicoa Street
Asheville, NC 28801
Telephone: 828/258 3939
www.fws.gov

U.S. Fish & Wildlife Service/ Charleston Field Office
176 Croghan Spur Road, Suite 200
Charleston, SC 29407
Telephone: 843/727 4707
www.fws.gov